Something Old

VINTAGE WEDDING DRESS FASHION LOOK BOOK

BY NANCY J. PRICE

More vintage fun from Synchronista!

Vintage Women: Adult Coloring Book series
#1: Classic art by Nell Brinkley
#2: Vintage Fashion from the Edwardian Era
#3: Vintage Fashion from the Early 1920s
#4: Victorian Fashion Scenes from the Late 1800s
#5: Victorian Fashion Plates from the Late 1800s
#6: Fashion from the Year 1916
#7: Vintage Fashion Layouts from the Early 1920s

Vintage Patterns: Adult Coloring Book: 44 beautiful nature-inspired vintage patterns from the Victorian & Edwardian eras

Dream of Time (a novel)

Also: Find thousands of articles & photos from the past at ClickAmericana.com

Something Old: Vintage Wedding Dress Fashion Look Book

Copyright © 2016 by Nancy J Price

This book features digitally-edited and restored versions of selected illustrations and photographs from the 1830s to the 1940s. While many of the originals are now in the public domain, this book collection, format and all copyrights to those derivative works are reserved by Synchronista LLC, thus the images herein may not be reproduced without express written permission.

Published by Synchronista LLC – Gilbert, Arizona, USA
Produced in partnership with ClickAmericana.com & Myria.com

Synchronista® and Click Americana®
are registered trademarks of Synchronista LLC
Synchronista.com

You are cordially invited ...

Inside this book, you'll find a collection of more than 300 images, documenting over a century of bridal fashions from the Western world! Find details about everything that went into preparing a bride for her walk down the aisle — from the tiara on her head to the toe of her shoe — and, of course, the all-important wedding dress.

The illustrations and photographs within cover eleven and a half decades between 1832 and 1947. They're presented chronologically so you can easily find a specific era, or simply browse the gowns, veils, hairstyles and bouquets to see how fashions changed through the years.

Every one of the authentic antique images in this book was carefully chosen, then digitally restored as much as possible to return them to their original glory.

Along with the images from vintage magazines and newspapers, we have included many of the descriptions originally published alongside them — including tips on fabrics, cuts, colors, trim, embellishments and accessories. With that insight, you can understand the trends behind the styles, and exactly what went into making each wedding dress design and bridal ensemble — meaning you can even try to recreate your favorite classic looks!

I hope you enjoy this little trip through time.

Best,

Nancy J. Price
Founder, Click Americana
Editor-in-Chief, Myria.com
Author, *Dream of Time*

VINTAGE FASHION TERMS

The older the outfit, the more foreign the terms used in the descriptions may seem. Here are a few definitions:

à deux jupes	French for "two skirts"
Crepe de Chine	Fine, gauzy crepe fabric
Fagoting	Decorative embroidery where threads are tied off in groups
French Val	Short for Valenciennes lace, a type of French lace dating from the 1700s
Guimpe	A high-necked starched blouse worn showing beneath a low-necked dress
Honiton	A type of famous English lace
Jabot	Lace frill or ruffle
Mode	French for "fashion"
Mousseline de soie	A lightweight silk muslin
Pelerine	A narrow cape
Ruche	Gathered, bunched or pleated fabric that creates a ruffled trim
Toilette/toilet	An outfit or clothing ensemble
Tulle	Fine mesh fabric — can be made from many thread types and in numerous w
Voile	Thin, semi-transparent fabric; French for "veil"

*Something old,
something new,
something borrowed,
something blue,
and a silver sixpence
in her shoe.*

~ ENGLISH FOLK RHYME

1832

The hair is in two high bows, wreathed together with a braid. Madonna bands on the forehead, and long ringlets at the side of the face. A lace scarf is arranged at the back of the hair, and falls on each side nearly as low as the hem of the dress.

The robe is of white net, with application of Honiton sprigs, arranged in a beautiful pattern on the chest, sleeves, and skirt. The corsage à la chemisette, cut to show the neck, somewhat lower than the throat, and edged with narrow lace.

The sleeves are not only of great fullness above the elbow, but are very large at the wrist. Scarf sash of white gauze satinée, tied in two bows in front with long ends, finished with silk tassels.

Under dress of white satin, with very large round sleeves at the upper arm; the corsage low at the bust. Bouquet of white roses and orange blossoms. Silk stockings of open work; shoes of white moiré. Four rows of large opals round the throat, opal bracelets and earrings.

Credit: The Lady's Magazine (and Museum), 1832

1838

The robe is of English lace over white satin, the skirt is trimmed with a very deep flounce; a corresponding one, but narrow, is arranged on the fronts and round the back of the skirt at some distance from the first, so as to have the appearance of a second robe

The corsage, pointed before and behind, is drooped on the bosom, and trimmed with a lace pelerine of a novel form.

The sleeve is tight from the shoulder to the wrist, but a double ruffle placed above the elbow, gives it an appearance of fullness.

The hair dressed low behind, and in full bands at the sides, is decorated with the bridal veil, white roses, orange flowers, and a fancy jewelery ferronière [headband].

Credit: The Ladies' Pocket Magazine, 1838

1840

Queen Victoria and Prince Albert seen after their marriage ceremony at St James's Palace in London, England, on February 10, 1840. At the time, she wrote in her journal: "I wore a white satin gown with a very deep flounce of Honiton [lace], imitation of old. I wore my Turkish diamond necklace and earrings, and Albert's beautiful sapphire brooch."

1845

Credit: (both pages) United States Library of Congress

1846

Bridal style from before the Civil War

As seen here, very similar bridal ensembles were depicted by two major lithographers — Currier and Sarony & Major — in 1846, likely reflecting the most popular fashions of the year.

Credit: Image on lower left by Nathaniel Currier | Image at upper right by Sarony & Major — both via the US Library of Congress.

The marriage morning

The marriage evening

Credit: Art by Nathaniel Currier, via the US Library of Congress. Date approximate.

1846

THE YOUNG BRIDE.

1853

(Above) The Empress of the French, in her bridal costume

Doña María Eugenia Ignacia Augustina de Palafox-Portocarrero de Guzmán y Kirkpatrick, 16th Countess of Teba and 15th Marchioness of Ardales, married French Emperor Napoleon III on January 29, 1853

1858

(Below) Dress à deux jupes of rich white glacèe silk, the first skirt being very long and full; the second skirt has side trimmings of broad blond set foot to foot with nœuds [ties] of satin ribbon in the center. Plain high body, with the point at waist slightly rounded; closed up the front with small pearl buttons set in gold. Blond bèrthe and collar. Short open sleeve trimmed with broad blond, and ornamented by a bow in the front of arm. Very full bouillon sleeves of tulle, with blond ruffle. Long veil of tulle fastened by a wreath of orange blossoms.

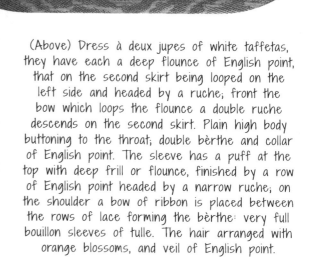

(Above) Dress à deux jupes of white taffetas, they have each a deep flounce of English point, that on the second skirt being looped on the left side and headed by a ruche; front the bow which loops the flounce a double ruche descends on the second skirt. Plain high body buttoning to the throat; double bèrthe and collar of English point. The sleeve has a puff at the top with deep frill or flounce, finished by a row of English point headed by a narrow ruche; on the shoulder a bow of ribbon is placed between the rows of lace forming the bèrthe; very full bouillon sleeves of tulle. The hair arranged with orange blossoms, and veil of English point.

Dress à deux jupes of white glacèe silk. The first skirt is plain, the second has four rows of Honiton lace forming tablière; they are put on in a zig-zag form and ornamented by white ribbon. The plain high body has the waist à pointe. Two rows of lace form a bè-the à coeur, the ends crossed and fastened by a bouquet of white roses. The sleeves are of the form styled Croates, being a wide pagoda, very short in the front of arm, trimmed with two rows of lace and bow of ribbon; collar of Honiton lace. Veil of plain tulle reaching nearly to the bottom of the dress, and wreath of white roses, jasmine and myrtle flowers.

1862

Credit: Godey's Lady's Book, 1862

1863

Princess Alexandra of Denmark married Queen Elizabeth's son, Albert Edward, Prince of Wales, in 1863. Albert became King Edward VII in 1902, making her the Queen-Empress consort of the United Kingdom.

Credit: United States Library of Congress

1874

Credit: The Peterson Magazine, Volumes 65-66, 1874

Princesse Dress (à deux jupes) of rich white silk. At the bottom of skirt is a fluted flounce partially covered by a flounce arranged in hollow pleats, alternated by spaces ornamented by buttons and elongated holes marked out by rouleaux.

Above the flounces, the front of skirt forms a large square tablier draped and edged by white lace headed by a double biais band; the back of skirt forms a deep square-shaped piece similarly edged.

The upper skirt and corsage form an open tunique à gilet, the gilet portion continuing across the shoulders and forming a point; the gilet closes by buttons and the sides of corsage and of tunique skirt (enclosing it) are edged by a double biais band and by white lace laid on flat.

In each corner of tunique-skirt are four buttons and elongated holes marked out by rouleaux: the sides are caught up and fastened by bows and short ends of white satin ribbon, the back of skirt being bouffant.

The neck is ornamented by a collar forming points in front, and edged by narrow lace with a biais band.

The sleeves have broad fancy cuffs ornamented by the buttons and imitated holes; the lower portions of cuffs form bands edged by narrow lace and fastened by single buttons. The figure is almost entirely enveloped by a veil of white tulle.

This elegant Wedding Robe is designed by Madame Breant Castel.

1878

Credit: The London and Paris Ladies' Magazine of Fashion, 1878

19

1881

Bride's dress of moire antique and satin, trimmed with rich lace. The body forms a point in front, and is princesse shaped behind; trimmed with lace and looped up by bunches of orange flowers. The front of body is opened en V, and trimmed with a jabot of lace and a spray of orange flowers. The underskirt is of gathered satin and bouillonnes, and trimmed by four lace flounces and a wreath of orange flowers. The body is laced up in front.

Credit: Townsend's Monthly Selection of Parisian Costumes (1881)

Bridal veils & headdresses

1885

Credit: Godey's Lady's Book

1887

Credit: Florence Folger – Married William A. Webster, 1887 – Courtesy of the Nantucket Historical Association | *Godey's Lady's Book*

When the bride wasn't in white

White wedding dresses only became truly in vogue after Queen Victoria chose a white bridal gown in 1840 (as seen on page 6). But for decades afterward, women still occasionally wore dark dresses to the altar, as these marriage portraits from the late 1800s show. In many cases, it wasn't a fashion statement, but a matter of practicality: the bride simply wore the finest dress she owned, often adding a traditional white bridal veil.

Wedding dresses worn by five White House brides

1820 Maria Monroe **1841** Elizabeth Tyler **1866** Harriet Lane **1874** Nellie Grant **1886** Frances Folsom Cleveland

Beginning in 1820, the first White House bride was Miss Maria Monroe. The Empire style still showed its influence in the short waist and straight, scant skirt. Over the simple gown of white satin was worn a little bodice of pale blue satin. This was finished at the bottom with little lace-trimmed tabs. Two simple fillets of silver were bound around the smoothly-parted hair, while a wreath of roses held the long veil in place.

Miss Elizabeth Tyler in 1841 wore a bridal gown which at that period was a marvel of beauty. An overdress of heavy white satin was fitted tightly to the figure above the waist, while the flaring skirt was slashed open in front to show an underskirt of palest lavender, trimmed with flounces of Brussels lace. The edges of the white overskirt were embroidered in silver. The sleeves showed ruffles of the same lace. Fastening the front of the bodice were silver-embroidered buttons with festoons of pearls.

The next wedding was in 1866, when Miss Harriet Lane wore the charming costume of that period. About her sloping shoulders were folds of white satin arranged so as to form a deep point in front. Beneath this the tight-fitting bodice was drawn down in like manner, while the stiffly supported, voluminous skirt puffed out like a balloon below it. Bands of the material, laid in narrow plaits, encircled the skirt, with a deep flounce of point lace at the bottom, caught by pink roses.

A wedding that is still remembered was that of Miss Nellie Grant in 1874. Her gown of white satin was made with long, tight-fitting bodice, having a vest of rare lace. The square neck was filled with a little frill of lace. About the hips was draped satin in heavy folds, which were drawn up at the back in an enormous mass of material from which hung the rather scant train. A deep ruffle of lace trimmed the bottom of the skirt. Her hair was dressed high, with a deep fringe in front, and sprays of orange blossoms were fastened in the veil.

When Miss Frances Folsom became the bride of President Cleveland in 1886, her gown of rich white satin was in the height of fashion. The long, perfectly-fitting bodice was lavishly trimmed with point lace and finished about the bottom with narrow folds of the material. These formed a broad band, which was further decorated by a garland of delicate pink roses. At the back, great folds of the satin fell from the high bustle, to form a long train. The veil, fastened with orange blossoms, was long enough in the back almost to cover the train. She carried no bouquet.

1895

The gown in the illustration is made of white satin trimmed with old lace, orange blossoms and white silk muslin. The cut is princess, forming a long train at the back, and the lower edge being trimmed all round with old lace.

The front of the skirt has two fluted folds beginning at some distance from the waist under a tiny bunch of the blossoms. The top of the bodice is filled in with a yoke of lace, bordered with draperies of white silk muslin coming from the shoulders.

The balloon sleeves are capped with lace-trimmed jockeys. Folded collar of silk muslin adorned with orange blossoms. The long veil is of Mechlin tulle fastened to the hair with a small wreath of orange blossoms.

Observe also the way in which the hair is dressed, as it is very effective.

Credit: The Morning Call, March 03, 1895 | Fort Worth Gazette, March 03, 1895

(Left) Wedding, traveling and bridesmaids' costumes

(Left) One of the latest bridal costumes designed by a famous house.

(Above) Railroad heiress Anna Gould married France's Count of Castellane in New York City in 1895

Credit: The San Francisco Call, March 24, 1895

1897

(Below)
Élièle et Rèbeka
South Africa

Credit: Eliele et Rebeka, groupe de maries, 1897 (Schomburg Center for Research in Black Culture, Jean Blackwell Hutson Research and Reference Division)

Credit: Omaha Daily Bee, January 03, 1897

1897

Credit: Godey's Lady's Book, 1897

(Center) Bridal gown of white satin. The trained skirt is trimmed with flounce of mousseline de soie, surmounted by a spray of orange flowers. The bodice is trimmed with a spray of the same. The sleeves are gathered their entire length and surmounted by two flounces of the mousseline. White tulle veil and white suede gloves.

(Left) White bengaline silk bridesmaid's costume. (Right) The bride's going away costume of fawn-colored cloth bordered with black embroidered ribbon, and Valenciennes lace with shaded green sequins.

1897

(Left)
Bridal toilette of
ivory white Duchesse
— Satin trimmed with
Brussels applique —
Rounded yoke of
drawn chiffon

Credit: New York Tribune, June 13/The Sun, May 09, 1897

The present fancy for the bridal bouquet is to have white half-opened roses, with their foliage mingled with smilax and maidenhair fern, and the whole tied with a tulle bow with long ends.

This exquisite robe of satin Duchesse has a corsage made in this form, embroidered and filled in by a low guimpe of mousseline de sole. Pleatings of the mousseline form a panel on the princess skirt.

Credit: The Times, September 19, 1897

1898

The reign of ribbons

Ribbons deserve a chapter to themselves. Saving the taffeta quality, that holds its own, and the liberty satin that has no rival, the most popular type is the transparent weave. Its variations in mesh and color are too numerous to be mentioned. There is coarse silk ribbon, with a satin edge. Grenadine ribbons are shot and edged with lace. Silk muslin ribbon, with a selvage, chiffon ribbon and ribbon that is finished in satin of one color on one side and moire of another color on the reverse, are all to be classed among novelties.

Credit: The Salt Lake Herald, March 27, 1898

(Right) Ivory white Irish poplin gown, daintily trimmed, fichu fashion, with chiffon. Ruffles of chiffon relieve the severity of the skirt. Orange blossoms, tulle veil and a shower bouquet make up a ravishing ensemble.

1899

(Below) This bridal gown of white satin has a bolero corsage and skirt with a glove-fitting tunic. The guimpe and vest are of gathered white mousseline de soie. Ruches of the same ornament all edges. The bridesmaid's gown is of pink taffeta with bands of gold embroidery.

A Polynesian bride

Queen Lavinia Veiongo, bride of Tonga's King Tupou II in 1899

Credit: The Anaconda Standard, October 10, 1899 | Queen Lavinia Veiongo by J. Martin; Image from the collections of the State Library of NSW, Australia

Credit: The Delineator [Magazine], 1899

1899

Silver belles

Credit: Kansas City Journal, June 11, 1899

(Left) The skirt, with its scanty shape above and its flare below, extends into a considerable train, and consists of a foundation of shimmering white taffeta, which is entirely veiled by white mousseline de soie and lace. At the front, the white mousseline is laid on in wide tucks which form V-shaped points, and with the alternate bands of exquisite lace, compose a tablier [apron]. The white taffeta of the train is covered with an all-over design of duchess point lace. The bodice is charmingly dainty and modest, and matches the skirt in its decorations as once rich and simple.

(Right) A very elaborate gown for a bride is of white satin embroidered in silver. The front is a solid mass of silver embroidery extending to a high point upon the skirt. The same embroidery is carried entirely around the train, which has no other trimming.

1900

The century turns!

(Right) Cashmere of a lustrous quality, almost as brilliant as silk, is used for bridal gowns. It is made up precisely as though it were the conventional satin. A lace yoke, lace sleeves and a lace veil give the finishing touches.

1900

Credit: The Delineator [Magazine], Volume 55 1900

(Opposite page on left) Ivory satin and all-over lace were here associated for the handsome wedding dress, which is richly adorned with pearl ornaments and passementerie and a double ruffle of embroidered chiffon. The waist has a fancy yoke-chemisette and a smooth back yoke. The full fronts are tucked at the arm hole, and caps give character to the shapely sleeves.

Wedding dresses of chiffon, lace & satin

(Opposite page on right) Dress made of Duchesse satin and tucked and plain chiffon, embellished with orange blossoms and chiffon ruches. The fronts of the waist are draped over the bust but are plain below, and the seamless back is smoothly stretched over the figure. The sleeves are finished by flaring cuffs, and a folded belt of satin finishes the waist.

Credit: From the Texas State Archives – Samuel Bell Maxey Collection. Elgie Crook Fairfax (1900)

Elgie Crook Fairfax of Texas, 1900

1900

A more charming bridal gown could scarcely be desired than the one here portrayed, developed in ivory white satin and all-over lace. Frills of lace, white satin ribbon and sprays of orange blossoms are employed as garniture.

The dress shows the faultless adjustment which distinguishes the princess modes. The fancy bolero, which contributes greatly to the attractiveness of the design, is gracefully curved to be quite shallow at the center of the back and caught up at the left side in front to produce a draped effect. The full-length sleeves are in this instance omitted, and the bolero sleeves are finished at their fancy lower edge with a frill of lace. Similar frills outline the bolero and are arranged about the bottom of the skirt, which may be made with a full-length or demi train.

The high stock is deepest at the sides, and the long tulle veil is held in place by a wreath of orange blossoms. Crepe de Chine and voile are also used for bridal toilettes, and would reproduce the mode prettily combined with accordion-plaited and tucked chiffon.

Credit (both pages): The Delineator [Magazine], November 1900

The rich fabrics associated in this gown, together with the perfect adjustment, make the mode one of marvelous beauty. Heavy white satin combined with all-over lace was used in the development, with ribbon, lace edging, chiffon ruchings and an artistic disposal of orange blossoms for garniture.

The dress is in princess style and closes at the back. Fullness is introduced below the waist-line at the center of the back and arranged in an underfolded double box-plait that falls into the long train, which may be in demi-length and have square or round corners. At the lower part of the front and side-front seams fan-plaited sections are introduced with good results. A high stock collar is at the neck, and the close-fitting two-seam sleeves are fancifully shaped at the wrist. A bolero is also included in the pattern, but in this instance is omitted.

The long tulle veil is secured under a wreath of orange blossoms. Satin Duchesse, bengaline or corded taffeta could be associated with Renaissance, Cluny or Irish point, with ruches of mousseline, Liberty silk and ribbon for garniture. A handsome gown of heavy white silk has a decoration of white satin ribbon and applique lace arranged over the seams.

Miss Mabel Davison
as she became
Mrs. Wray Bentley

Credit: Daily Inter Mountain (Butte, Montana), June 23, 1900 | Family of Mrs. Wray A. Bentley

(Below) A chiffon and lace bridal gown, made over a body of white silk. A complete gown of white taffeta is closely-fitted, and over it is draped tulle, mousseline de soie or chiffon.

Gowns for brides keep pace with the fashions. You see the new sleeves, the sloping shoulders and the draped front.

The skirt is tight-fitting around the hips and full around the foot. Necks are worn high, though it is permissible to cut them down as low as the throat.

1901

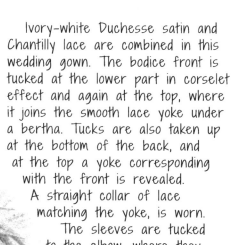

Ivory-white Duchesse satin and Chantilly lace are combined in this wedding gown. The bodice front is tucked at the lower part in corselet effect and again at the top, where it joins the smooth lace yoke under a bertha. Tucks are also taken up at the bottom of the back, and at the top a yoke corresponding with the front is revealed.

A straight collar of lace matching the yoke, is worn. The sleeves are tucked to the elbow, where they terminate in a puff, and a facing of the lace is applied to the lower part. A belt closing with a handsome buckle and a bunch of white roses arranged on the left of the corsage give the finishing touches essential to a gown of this style. A panel effect of the lace is arranged on the trained seven-gored skirt, which has a becoming flare at the foot.

At the back, box-plaited fullness is introduced, falling with graceful effect into the long train, and a ruche of chiffon follows the lower edge. The tulle veil is caught up with the conventional orange blossoms, and a bunch of bride roses.

"The bride's robe is a most graceful one, fashioned of white crepe de chine lining over white taffeta. Duchess lace forms the trimming of this gown. The crepe de chine is dotted over with tiny pearl beads, producing an effect that is both new and beautiful. The pearl beads are far prettier than the embroidered dots, and I may say here that the sewing of both pearl and crystal beads on soft and silky fabrics is a notion that is becoming very popular with makers of the most fashionable and original costumes. The veil that this pretty young bride will wear is of India lace. This lace is of a very fine texture, the net used for a foundation being almost as light as tulle."
— Marie Armstrong

Credit The St Louis Republic, May 26, 1901

1902
What the most fashionable brides wear

The average bridal gown is a mean between the rich simplicity of a year ago, and the elaborate that preceded it. White satin lace and mousseline de soie over satin are the most exploited fabrics. Silk gowns are never worn by really fashionable brides, and gems are no longer countenanced. Flowers are substituted in the hair and on the corsage.

Credit: The Saint Paul Globe, May 25, 1902

Credit: The San Francisco Call, April 06, 1902

1902

Ruffles & puffs

(Right) Some of her petticoats may be combinations of lace edging, insertion and ruffles of the sheer cambric, others may be embroidery and ruffles. The embroidery, like the lace, however, should be dainty and delicate. Around the top of the ruffles, ribbon is run in a beading of white and tied in a bow at one side.

(Above) The dress is made of white chiffon and cream lace over white satin. The waist has a tucked yoke, with a full front and a short bolero of the lace. The sleeves, which are also of the lace, only reach the elbow, where they are finished off with triple frills. The skirt has a front panel of the lace, and the full overskirt of chiffon is decorated with soft puffings around the bottom.

Credit: The Salt Lake Herald, August 24, 1902 | The Kalispell Bee, March 01, 1902

Credit: The Salt Lake Herald, April 20, 1902

1903

Incorporating Irish lace

(Left) Ivory-white crepe de Chine was here united with Irish point lace. The skirt is shirred at the top and again some distance below, the shirrings terminating to form a narrow front panel covered with the lace, and a long sweep is introduced.

(Right) This bride is gowned in white chiffon foulard elaborately offset with Belgian lace. The bodice is closed at the back and pouches in the approved manner in front. The circular Monte Carlo bolero with cap sleeves is composed entirely of lace, and is topped by a standing collar. A wide, soft girdle is crushed about the waist, and the full sleeves of the bodice are lengthened by close lace portions with mitt wrists.

This charming bridal gown (above left), waist and skirt are combined, lace and handmade motifs elaborating the ivory silk mousseline.

This dainty toilette for a bridesmaid (above right) unites a waist and skirt; pale pink chiffon cloth was trimmed with chiffon frills and feather stitching.

This bridal toilette in white liberty satin is elaborated with all-over tucking, Irish point lace and orange blossoms.

1904

Wedding gowns are no longer stately and stiff, as satins have given place to soft, filmy materials. Mousseline de soie with leaves of white lace and orange blossoms of pearls now form the smartest bridal attire. Wedding veils will hereafter be looped with orange blossoms, and white and green are the spring colors.

Credit: The Washington Times, April 17, 1904

"You must be picturesque to be fashionable."

The festoon flounce, which has been revived along with other Louis modes, is seen upon a large number of the new wedding gowns, and affords a good opportunity for the artistic use of handsome lace.

1904

1904

The look of fine needlework

(Above) The bridal waist is severely high in the throat, for the least degree of decolletage is considered indecorous. But a low cut will often be simulated in many ways, and then filled in with a high lace guimpe or yoke of some sort.

Credit: Evening Star (Washington DC), September 17, 1904 | The San Francisco Call, April 03, 1904.

(Below) Upon a gown of white satin de Lyons, a chain of orange blossoms is looped with bows into Louis XV garlands. The low-cut bodice is shirred at sleeves, bust and back, and filled in with a yoke of Duchesse lace. Two frills of the same lace fall below one of the sleeves, which are elaborately puffed and trimmed down the shirring with orange blossoms.

(Above) The charming gowns here illustrated were designed for The American Dressmaker by Mme. Baker, the famous fashion expert. Figure 1 is a gown for a matron of honor. Figure 2 is a wedding gown of ivory chiffon cloth with shirred skirt, fichu and puffed elbow sleeves of same. Trimming: Flounces, galons, bolero, frills and yoke of point Alencon lace. Figure 3 is a bridesmaid's toilette.

1905

The princesse gown affords rich opportunity for lace trimming. The simple, graceful lines of the waist show off to great advantage the broad, deep yoke and the beruffled elbow.

Walking down the aisle

Credit: Evening Star (Washington DC), October 22, 1905

1905

Behold the brides

Credit: The Saint Paul Globe, April 16, 1905

(Right) Eleanor Roosevelt, the longest-serving First Lady of the United States, seen wearing her wedding dress in New York City, 1905, upon her marriage to President Franklin D. Roosevelt.

Eleanor later became the first Chairperson of the Presidential Commission on the Status of Women, and the first Chairperson of the United Nations Commission on Human Rights.

Credit: Evening Star (Washington DC), April 15, 1905 | Eleanor Roosevelt wearing her wedding dress in New York City, 1905

1906

(Left) The newest bridal gowns are cut on princess lines, and some of them differ in a marked degree from the close-fitting effects with which we have of late become familiar. The sheath-like skirt is retained, but it narrows in more sharply from hip-line to knee, and swirls out below with greater fullness than ever.

(Right) The bridal veil may be of tulle or real lace.

For the fashionable wedding gown, satin is the material par excellence.

1906

Ways to wear the wedding veil

72

Credit: Los Angeles Herald., May 13, 1906 | Los Angeles Herald., December 30, 1906

Bridal bouquets

1906

June brides

A) Wedding gown of embroidered mull panels, trimmed with lace and medallions.

B) Lingerie wedding gown of sheer lawn, trimmed with two kinds of lace and raised hand embroidery.

LACE PANEL ON SKIRT B

Credit: The Washington Times, June 03, 1906

74

1907

Cream liberty satin was used for this model [in the middle], the trimming being of Brussels lace forming a fichu. The yoke was of hand-tucked chiffon and lace, and the sleeves had graceful little caps of satin and lace. The high girdle, which was drawn up in Empire effect in the back, was of the material, and the train was very long and sweeping. A cluster of orange blossoms was arranged where the fichu crossed in front, just a few inches above the belt, and on the head was worn a coronet of orange blossoms, beneath which the tulle veil was arranged.

Credit: Los Angeles Herald, October 27, 1907

1907

One point to be remember is that no matter how intricate the detail and trimming of the bridal gown, its outline should be of severe simplicity. The charm of the bridal veil is decidedly marred when it falls over a gown with too many frills and furbelows, while nothing is more charming than a graceful clinging robe, defining the figure in unbroken lines under a floating tulle or lace veil.

Credit: Los Angeles Herald, May 26, 1907

A beautiful gown of mousseline de soie, with a court train of lace trimmed with orange blossoms

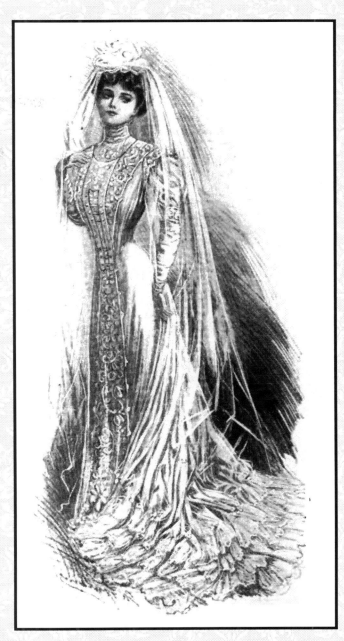

Shirred bodices are very becoming to slender figures, and the long train is traditional.

The Easter bride will wear empire or princess gowns of satin, trimmed with diaphanous lace. More lace and silver embroidery are used upon wedding gowns than ever before, and court trains and chiffon trimmings and linings are usual with wedding gowns this season.

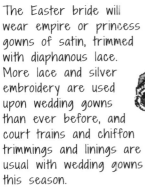

The Easter Bride

A) The wedding gown is modified empire effect, built of satin Duchesse.

B) The bride's receiving gown of apricot pink chiffon with gold trimmings.

C) The bride's wedding dress converted into a dinner gown. Showing the front of the gown.

D) The bride's afternoon reception gown of rose satin draped with lace.

1907

The princess lines are extremely effective in bridal gowns, and are much favored.

(Far right) A precious lace heirloom frequently replaces the conventional tulle veil.

(Right) A graceful wedding gown of ivory white silk. The guimpe is made of Duchesse lace, and the sleeve flounces are of Duchesse and point lace combined. The jumper has a turnover collar of hand embroidery, which makes it very unique. It has three tucks on each shoulder front and back to give the desired fullness. The kimono sleeves and front are also hand-embroidered. The skirt is made plain, nine gores, with full sweep or round length as preferred.

1908

Two bridal gowns

One is made of beautiful Swiss embroidery, using three flounces for the skirt, and the same embroidery is used in fashioning the waist. A soft sash girdle of silk covers the joining of the upper and lower parts. This dress is also useful for many other times and can be dry cleaned or laundered.

The other is of softest satin with a simple over drapery of sheer with a narrow embroidered edge. If a veil is to be worn, there is nothing prettier than tulle, as it falls so softly and lightly.

Credit: The San Francisco Call, December 06, 1908

Formal toilette of chiffon and silk

Credit: The San Francisco Call, April 26, 1908 | Los Angeles Herald, March 29, 1908

Brides' gowns of white satin embroidered with silver and pearls

1909

Take a plain white net. Make it slightly high-waisted and give it a princess effect by extending the panel front of the skirt up to the shallow yoke depth. Use German valenciennes insertion to outline the panel front, and whip a tiny edge to the outside edge of the insertion.

The skirt part should be fastened to the raised belt, and the fullness laid in small tucks, extending a hip depth. There must be enough fullness in the blouse so that a scant look is avoided, but naturally there must be no blousing. The sleeves may be long or finished just below the elbow, and the neck with a high collar of the lace.

Credit: The San Francisco Call, May 02, 1909

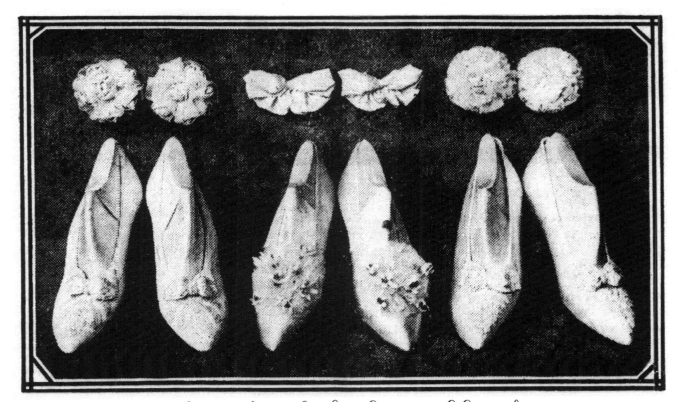

~ Dainty things for the bride: Wedding footwear ~

The bridal footwear means another considerable item of expense. Of course, no self-respecting bride would walk to her new estate in anything but the daintiest of shoes or slippers, and beneath the snowy satin wedding frock must be footwear in keeping.

Equally, of course, it would be a pity to shame such pretty slippers with any stockings but those of finest silk. Bridal hose of cobwebby thread silk, hand embroidered with white flowers and bow knots, are to be had from seven to twenty-five dollars the pair, though, of course, ordinary plain silk sorts may be bought for more modest prices. The pure white stocking, of all others, must be infinitely fine, and $10. after all, is a trifle to lay for the hose one walks to happiness in.

When it comes to the bridal slippers, no woman expects to spare expense, and well the crafty storekeeper knows it, for some of the prices set on bridal slippers would make the prospective husband feel positively faint. Three charming styles in wedding slippers are shown in the picture: two pairs of satin, and the third pair of beaded buckskin, and for these pretty slippers the bride may choose her own style of bow, buckle or rosette.

Beaded buckskin slippers are considered smart just now, but there is about a century-old sentiment that clings about the little satin wedding shoes, and most brides prefer them. The beaded satin slippers are more expensive than the plain-toed sort, but are scarcely prettier than the dainty plain-toed pair shown with puffed tulle rosettes, in which nestle orange blossoms.

1910

The bride's gown of heavy white satin is cut en princesse, and the square yoke of dotted net is draped on each side with princess lace in fichu fashion. The lace veil, reaching to the knees, is prettily arranged on top of the head with orange blossoms.

Credit: The Ogden Standard, January 25, 1910

Credit: The San Francisco Call, October 16, 1910

1910

When She Marries in Holiday Time

Bridal Veil with Ribbon Band and Rosette of Ribbon and Roses

White Satin Bridal Gown, Embroidered in White Silk — Veil of Tulle Decorated with Rose Wreath

The first question of importance after the bridal robe has been decided upon is "How shall I wear my veil?"

Recent brides have discovered a new plan of draping it, so that the upper part of the lace forms a close fitting cap with ends either long or short hanging from it.

There seems to be no so-called happy medium. The veil must fall either to the edge of the hem of the gown, or must be exceedingly short.

The value of the cap arrangement is that the coiffure need not be disarranged after the marriage ceremony, as it almost invariably is when the veil is worn over the face. Many of these lace veils are mounted over tulle, for not only does the tulle soften the lace, but it also gives to it the little crispness that is missing in old lace.

In arranging the cap, the tulle is mounted on a small wire with one end of the cap wider than the other. This method simplifies draping. When, however, the lace is in scarf or shawl shape it is better to use it as an overdrapery for the tulle veil. Except in the panel arrangement, the veil should never extend quite to the end of the train, but stop at the edge of the hem.

In regard to the bridal wreath, the spiked tiara of the orange blossoms and myrtle foliage has finally departed after a long reign of popularity. There has arrived in its place a small hat wreath, in some instances encircling the head completely, and in others ending halfway around it.

ONE OF THE NEW SHORT BRIDAL VEILS IN PRINCESS LACE, CAUGHT WITH A SPRAY OF ORANGE BLOSSOM

PLACE CARDS FOR THE HOLIDAY WEDDING THE BRIDE IN WHITE, BRIDESMAID IN PINK. CUPID UNDER THE PARASOL IN WHITE, PINK AND GREEN. CUPID IN SLIPPERS WITH ORANGE BLOSSOMS, WEDDING BASKET, WHITE AND GREEN. EACH CARD BEARS THE GUEST'S NAME.

BRIDAL VEIL OF TULLE, WITH WREATH OF ROSES

1910

Credit: The San Francisco Call, May 15, 1910

White satin wedding gowns: One with embroidered satin fichu, and the other with guimpe and sleeves of embroidered silver net.

1910

Beautiful brides ♡

Arranging the Veil

Arranging the Bridal Veil

For the bridal veil, lace or tulle may be used — old lace or new — or a happy combination of tulle with lace. In length, the veil is extravagant and follows the line of the train as it falls. The folds rest upon the shoulders or depend from the back, according to the face and figure of the wearer. The statuesque woman may carry to good effect the long, dignified folds covering the back only.

Little roses are a late Parisian fancy in flowers, but the wreath takes on whatever flower or form is necessary, so that every women may look her best upon her wedding day.

1911

Gowns with half-length sleeves

Credit: The Washington Herald, April 09, 1911

The bridal robe shown in the illustration of pearl white satin charmeuse is much in the mode of the bridal gown of Lady Decies [socialite Elizabeth Wharton Drexel]. It is semi-Empire, the skirt mounted on the bodice above the normal waist line. Sections of Duchesse lace, cut with deep points, encrust the front of the bodice and the skirt and are veiled with white chiffon. The neck is outlined with a band embroidered with silver and seed pearls. A similar band confines the slight fullness of the chiffon at the knees. The bretelles on the bodice are prolonged into bands which decorate the sides of the skirt. These bands show a design of lilies-of-the-valley embroidered in silver and seed pearls. The back gores, which form a square train, slope to the front where they are slightly draped over a band of Duchesse lace. The drapery is clasped by a small garland of orange blossoms. Above the lace cuff the sleeve is clasped by a cluster of orange blossoms.

1911

Much ado about mousseline

Bridesmaid's frock of mousseline with a silk jacket, and a bride's gown of white satin, mousseline and lace

Credit: The Sun (New York, NY), April 16, 1911

1912

A bridal gown of lace & satin

Credit: Evening Star (Washington DC), May 19, 1912

1913

President Woodrow Wilson's daughter, Jessie Woodrow Wilson, married Francis Bowes Sayre, Sr. on November 25, 1913.

For the summer bride

(Above center)
The gown is of white chiffon cloth, dropped over thin white lining satin. It has a draped tunic falling over a deep flounce of light shadow lace, and there is a bodice of the same length drawn around the bust and caught with a cluster of flowers in front. There is no train, and the veil, which is of white tulle, hangs to the hem of the skirt. The slippers are of white satin, and the bridal bouquet is a shower of white flowers held with loops of white satin ribbon.

Two attractive ways of draping the bridal veil

1913

The bridesmaid & bride in very modern costume

Credit: New York Tribune, May 25, 1913 | The Sun (New York, NY), March 16, 1913

Credit: New York Tribune, May 25, 1913

1914

White taffeta is the material used, with handsome silk-run lace for the vestee and rolling collar. The round-length skirt has a charmingly modest and graceful bustle drapery, especially becoming to the youthful bride. For the veil, white tulle is especially pretty, draped from a coronet of orange blossoms.

(Below) Wedding gown of white satin trimmed with rare old lace and draped with tulle

Beautiful ways to drape the bridal veil

1914

White charmeuse wedding gown, with corsage, veil & trimming of rose point

Credit: New York Tribune, March 22, 1914

(Right) The slightly bloused waist has the prevailing narrow-shouldered effect, and the two flower-petal collars, one of satin and the other of fine Limerick lace of the same variety which cascades gracefully over the modestly-exposed throat, down to the waistline in front. The long sleeves are very fine, white net and are ruffled to the wrist after the fashion of thirty years ago, while the novelty of the skirt lies in the broad, bias fitted piece which, wound from the waist in a slanting line around the hips, confines the fullness at the knees after the approved fashion of the moment.

1914

Credit (both pages) The Delineator [Magazine], Volume 84 – 1914

1915

(Below) Suffragette Genevieve Clark, daughter of [House of Representatives] speaker Champ Clark, married James McIllhany Thomson of New Orleans in Bowling Green, Missouri, on June 30, 1915.

Credit: El Paso Herald, May 22, 1915, | The Day Book, June 30, 1915

Graceful gown

The wedding gown shown is a copy of a Callot model, but with some slight modifications. It makes a very graceful bridal gown.

1916

For the June bride

A heavy white brocade overdress edged with orange blossoms. The petticoat of white tulle falls over an underskirt of lace. Undersleeves of silver tulle are veiled with lace that forms a cape in the back. Long train of the brocade.

Trousseau dress: Large patterned white lace flounces are over a petticoat of orchid and yellow taffeta. Lace bodice has glimpse of white tulle and sash of yellow and orchid ribbons.

Credit: Harper's Bazar, 1916

(Below) The charming bride pictured wears a val-edged net veil shirred into a wreath of lilies of the valley, forming a coronet headpiece. The gown is of white liberty satin, featuring a short full skirt with front panel, and elaborate court train of princess lace bordered with rich pearl embroidery. the neck is quite low, while the sleeves are the new bell shape, dropping to the wrist.

(Above) Veil of tulle, flesh pink in color. The edges are scalloped with a soft silver ribbon, and the same ribbon is snappily bowed at the wreath, with the ends wandering away and running the full length of the veil, only to be caught by a dainty little bunch of orange blossoms.

1916

(Upper right)
"Notice, if you please, the charm of my Catholic bride; with the soft clouds of 'white wind' framing her face and head, and veiling the spray of orange blossoms. Is this not the picture the personification of purity?"
— Fashion designer Herman Patrick Tappé

(Right) Best of all my fancies, none pleases me more than my syringa [lilac] hat, which is just a big floppy Leghorn with a band of pale green velvet ribbon and a wondrous plume of syringas, the orange blossoms of the north." — Tappé

Credit: Harper's Bazar (1916)

White wind

"Misty white tulle is not only symbolic of mystery, the bewitching purity of the bride, but enhances her beauty, and my feeling is to always enwrap her in filmy, beautifying folds of this white wind." — Tappé

Credit: Harper's Bazar (1916)

1916

Credit: US Library of Congress of Mrs. Henry Morgenthau, née Elinor Fatman

Shorter dresses becoming fashionable

1916

(Below) Wedding gown with motif of thread lace combined with faille silk. The tiny bit of veiling over the eyes is all that the new voluminous veil can spare as a hiding place for the bride's proverbial timidity.

(Below) Pointed overskirts and pointed trains that fall from the sides of the skirt are the motif of this bride's gown of white silk with lace insets and under-flounces.

(Above) Demureness is in every line of this heavy faille silk wedding gown, down to the ruffled cuffs of its tight silk sleeves.

Credit: New York Tribune, March 26, 1916

"Fairest of the flowers is the June bride, whose shimmering presence in garden, drawing room or sanctuary dwindles the glory of the proudest blossoms. June-time is bride-time. Society conspires to lavish homage on the feminine figure in the bridal group. The spotlight of curious, enthralled and reverent attention falls on the robed figure of the girl who is taking the wife's vows."

1917

Styles as the United States entered World War 1

Bridal gown of white satin, showing the barrel influence in the skirt. The bodice is simple and veiled with silk net, this being with pearls. The veil is of tulle edged with French val.

Credit: (Both pages) Richmond Times-Dispatch, July 11, 1917

Striking wedding dress featuring full ruffled skirt of net top lace with over-dress of white satin. The long veil is of rose point lace caught with orange blossoms.

Especially graceful is this bride's gown of white liberty satin, developed on loose lines and trimmed with lace and pearl passementerie. Tulle veil and orange blossoms.

1918

Veil Vogue

There are many ways of draping the veil. One very good way is to gather the tulle into a band of silver lace to form a close-fitting cap. Another is arranged in a larger cap with double frill about the face — as shown in the picture — and a third presents the veil falling from a coronet of fine lace, wired to hold it into position.

Credit: Mohave County Miner, July 13, 1918

(Below) Here is sketched one of the loveliest bridal gowns of the season. The gown begins with a foundation of white satin. The frock itself is of tulle and duchess lace, the lace hanging in a deep flounce from waist to hem. The surplice of the blouse is edged with tiny ruffles of pleated and net, and shows small net puff sleeves emerging from beneath elbow-length sleeves of satin.

1919

Wedding gown of white satin and white tulle veil. The sleeves and yoke are also tulle. A wide girdle of the satin is heavily embroidered in silver, and forms the panel train.

Credit: The Sun (New York, NY), February 16, 1919

How to arrange the wedding veils

One of the most charming arrangements of the lace veil is one that suggests the way a Spanish lady arranges her white lace mantilla... It is laid over the simply-arranged coiffure, and folds of the lace hang down on the shoulders, and the longer folds about the back. It is held slightly away from the face at the temples, but the fastening is invisible. — One of the smartest arrangements consists of a wide bandeau made of artificial orange blossoms that holds in place a puff crown of tulle. — Another interesting arrangement suggests a nun's wimple. The veil is puffed over the hair, and a soft folding of tulle is arranged around the chin and neck and drawn up to meet the veil. A band of orange flowers or of pearls is sometimes placed across the forehead.

1919

For post-war weddings

The American bride turns away from convent simplicity and looks to Paris for inspiration. There are many sources for suggestions for bridal veils, among them the headdresses of Brittany and Normandy.

White satin wedding gown with front and back panels of silver brocade, outlined with a border of pearls and silver. The bridesmaid's dress is of orchid-colored chiffon, with the apron effect made by loops of orchid-colored ribbon. At the waist is a cluster of unusual handmade silk flowers in shades that blend with the color of the frock. Hat of orchid crepe and very pale yellow roses. Wedding dress and veils from Maison Jacqueline. Bridesmaid's dress by Miss Carroll.

Credit (both pages): New York Tribune, May 04, 1919

A Brittany cap of lace and embroidered batiste, with tulle draped from the top of it, is used for the bride. Bridesmaid's leghorn hat covered with pale pink Georgette crepe and trimmed with two ostrich flats and little bunches of flowers. The lower bridesmaid wears a French blue hat of Neapolitan straw.

The high-draped bridal veil completely covers the face, and the folds of the drapery are caught a little above the ears with orange blossoms and gardenias. For the first bridesmaid, two pale pink ostrich flats are artistically draped over the crown of the orchid-colored straw hat. The second bridesmaid's hat is of old blue straw with jade green ostrich.

1920

Top modes of the twenties

(Right) Actress Billie Burke (later best known for playing Glinda in "The Wizard of Oz") in an ad for John Heathcoat & Co. bridal veils.

(Below) Edith Thornton favors a gown entirely of rare rose point lace, with a veil of the same costly material, wired to form a graceful fan arrangement — an alluring frame for the wearer's piquant brunette beauty.

(Above) Beatrice Joy's bridal dress of Georgette crepe is a marvel of simplicity and refinement, boasting no other trimming than deep, hand-run tucks and fine garlands of orange blossoms on skirt, decolletage and veil arrangement.

1920

(Above left) Bride's dress of accordion pleated silk tulle, having an apron panel front made of a succession of narrow pleats ending in sun-ray rosettes. (Second from left) Lace bridal dress of Oriental form made over a foundation of pleated tulle. (Far right) A typical French wedding gown with high neck and long sleeves.

(Left) Gown by Lanvin of Paris. It has a triple skirt of lace flounces and white satin. The long bodice is of satin. The train of lace drops from the shoulders.

1920 — Society brides

MRS. PHILIP S. P. RANDOLPH, JR., FORMERLY MISS MADELEINE COCHRANE.

Credit: Bride c1920 from the Frances Benjamin Johnston Collection | The Sun and the New York Herald, May 16, 1920

MRS. SCHUYLER LIVINGSTON PARSONS
FORMERLY MISS BETTY B. PIERSON
NOW WITH HER HUSBAND IN PARIS.

MRS. DANIEL DUKE THOMSON
WHO WAS MISS CONSTANCE EUGENIA SMITH

1920

Credit: Bisbee Daily Review, April 04, 1920

Washington Brides of the Season

All photographs by Harris & Ewing.

Mrs. Richard F. Wood, formerly Miss Ida Harry   Mrs. Edward P. Wroth, formerly Miss Marjorie Hamil   Mrs. Arthur E. Dowell, formerly Miss Louise E. Adams

Credit: Evening Star (Washington DC), July 04, 1920

1920

Mrs. Raymond Weisbrodt, formerly Miss Mildred Ralph

Mrs. John B. Carter, formerly Miss Celina Calvo

Mrs. Charles E. Pendergast, formerly Miss Marjorie Simpson

Mrs. Joseph Dolan, formerly Miss Rosemary Sweetman

1921

Lovely lace

(Left) Lace, the traditional and exquisite requisite of the bridal gown, can be used with satin, charmeuse or taffeta when a straight skirt of it veils a straight foundation skirt.

(Right) With that soft stateliness in mind that is so necessary beneath the picturesque sweep of the bridal veil, Paris designed this beautifully draped front tunic for crepes, crepe de Chine, crepe satin, crepe meteor, charmeuse and taffeta. The slipover waist has a camisole lining.

Credit: The Delineator [Magazine], 1921

At the forefront of fashion

(Above) J. H. Gidding's bridal outfit, with attendants, made one of the most notable exhibits at the fashion show of the Nations in New York City.

1921

(Left) Just enough stateliness to satisfy tradition and the smartest lines of the season Paris put into this lovely bridal gown made with a deep yoke and soft front tunic. The back is cut in one piece and there is a French body lining.

(Right) Charming short-skirted frock. Its soft, full lines are very lovely under a generous sweep of veil. The surplice waist, which is cut rather long, ties into a hip sash.

The season of simplicity

Credit: The Delineator [Magazine], 1921

Today, the keynote of the wedding gown is simplicity. The days of elaborate gowns with trains so heavy with the weight of precious jewels that eight girls had to carry them is over. The sensible American bride knows that simplicity is more becoming to the solemn dignity of the occasion than extremely elaborate dress.

From a study of the descriptions of bridal gowns at recent important weddings, we find that satin is without doubt the favorite material. Crepe de Chine and heavy white brocade are also used, and the bride may select whichever material she likes best — something soft and clinging unless she is inclined to be too slender, when taffeta is more suitable.

Undoubtedly, no matter what the style of gown happens to be, it should boast a train. White satin slippers and white gloves enhance the simple beauty of the wedding gown. Jewels are rarely worn, except, perhaps, one large gem — a gift of the groom.

1922

(Right) This gown is pure white Georgette fashioned over silver cloth that shimmers elusively like a summer cloud. Crystal beads ornament the entire garment, here and there a motif of crystal and pearl beads, the entire front panel being of that formation. The long train is of finest satin crepe suspended from the neckline. A long spray of white flowers with silvered stems forms the floral touch so indispensable to a bridal gown.

(Left) A full-court train outlined and ending with a heavy encrustation of pearls and beautifully embroidered. The bridal veil of tulle, which continues the full length, completes the ensemble.

1922

(Above) Mlle. Marguerite de Montgolfier, bride of Baron Roger de Longuerue, wears a gown of chiffon velvet over silver and a draped tulle veil.

Credit: (both pages) Vogue, 1922

(Left) At her wedding to the Count de Leusse, Mlle. Kulp shaped her crown of orange blossoms into the form of a diadem.

Mlle. Baudry, the bride of M. Jean Besnard, abandons orange blossoms and chooses in their place a kokoshnik of pearls.

(Left) The wedding coiffure of today scorns tradition and seeks individuality. Thus Mlle. Gisele Cahen-Fuzier completes her Botticelli gown with a veil of Florentine draping and a crown of silver laurel leaves.

1922

Slender and delicate in its crystalline tracery, this wedding gown gives an effect of snowflakes poised against white marquisette. The marquisette and satin of the train are joined by a lovely crystal embroidery matching the bandeau, which holds the veil of white tulle.

Credit: (both pages) Vogue, 1922

A new era of elegance

(Right) The panels and girdles of this supple white satin wedding gown are sewn with pearls, which are also used to outline the simply-cut neckline. The fine veil of needlepoint is caught with orange blossoms.

1922

Past and present meet in the brocade and silver cloth of this beautiful wedding gown designed by Poiret especially for the marriage of his niece. The long-waisted bodice of silver brocade falls over the full, gathered skirt of silver cloth in rounded points both in the front and the back. The sleeves display a delightful originality in being shirred to a deep shoulder line, and East meets West when the Occidental bride winds the long tulle veil into a turban about her head.

When one crosses the threshold of matrimony and the thirties simultaneously, one might wear this powder blue crepe romaine and silver lace frock. The headdress of pearls and silver cloth suggests and afternoon wedding, through the gown may serve for an evening ceremony.

In the fullness of life, one might look very slender in a grey crepe romaine wedding gown with length of line given by sleeve draperies and a panel, girdle and cuffs embroidered in platinum-colored pearls. A black Spanish lace veil accents the trim silhouette of the grey crepe hat.

1922

Shimmer & color

(Left) Peach-colored organdie, just a breath of it, applied to matching net in designs of flowers and foliage to make a lovely bridesmaid's frock. The bodice and part of the sleeves and long bouffant skirt are plain peach-colored organdie. The hat is of chartreuse-colored tulle.

(Above) Perhaps the ladies of the Empire wore ivory satin gowns as lovely as this, but it is difficult to believe. The little Empire bodice is outlined by tiny green leaves and pearls; shimmering loops of pearls festoon the gown. Panels of tulle fall from the close tulle headdress.

(Right) A slim, classically-draped gown of white crepe de Chine, with a rippling side train, and embroidered it all over with a shining pattern of little rings of mother-of-pearl. A bit of white chiffon was used to fill in the low corsage. The whole gown is opalescent and shimmering.

(left) Cut like a Chinese coat of fine white batiste, embroidered all over with wreaths and flowers, as finely wrought as if some industrious spider had done it, this frock is worn over a flesh-colored slip, and girdled with a wide sash of green ribbon that shows rather faintly through the white of the batiste.

1922

At the recent wedding of Mrs. Cromwell Brooks and Brigadier-General Douglas MacArthur, the wedding gown was a happy combination of peach chiffon and cream color Bruges lace. Softly-draped chiffon veiled the lace of the straight slip and floated in airy draperies from the sleeves, while long chiffon panels edged with Bruges lace made a double train. White camellias fell in a long spray from the wide girdle.

Credit: (both pages) VOGUE magazine, 1922

Slim and lovely in its white satin simplicity, this wedding gown is adorned by rows of pearls at the low waistline, and delicate embroidery of seed pearls and orange blossoms on the tulle sleeves. A bandeau of orange blossoms and a piquant fan effect at the head are unusual features of the veil.

1922

The bride and her attendants

Credit: The Ogden Standard-Examiner, May 21, 1922

157

1922

The wedding of Miss Katherine Mackay, daughter of Mr. Clarence H. Mackay [the socially-prominent financier and head of the Postal Telegraph Cable Company], to Mr. O'Brien, son of Mr. and Mrs. Morgan J. O'Brien, took place at Roslyn, Long Island. [Her mother was socialite and suffragette Katherine Alexander Duer Mackay.]

Credit: (Both pages) Harper's Bazar, 1922

Mrs. Charles J. Coulter, Jr., who was Miss Helen Lispenard Stewart Trevor, daughter of the Henry Graff Trevors, was perhaps the most interesting bride of the season. Her marriage brought together representatives of many old New York families, for she is connected with the Stewarts, the Rhinelanders and the Winthrops.

1922

PAINTED BY COLES PHILLIPS

Credit: (both pages) VOGUE magazine, 1922

1925

Now Mr & Mrs!

Wedding portraits

1933

Credit: United States Library of Congress • private collections (dates estimated)

1934

The love of a lifetime

Magdalene and George Robinson were married on June 23, 1934, in San Francisco

Credit: Private collection

1935

1936

All in white

1937

Christmas – Bateman
Wedding
March 20, 1937

Jason – Petigorsky
Wedding
May 30, 1937

Giroux – Ogilvie
Wedding
May 1, 1937

Credit: All photos on thee two page courtesy Library and Archives Canada (Yousuf Yousuf. Yousuf Karsh fonds. Library and Archives Canada)

Studio portraits of five beautiful brides

Mahoney – Brady
Wedding
April 10, 1937

Blackburn – Coristine
Wedding
April 29, 1937

1939

Wedding of Naomi and Al Fischer December 25, 1939

Credit: Naomi and Al Fischer on their wedding day, December 25, 1939 – Photo courtesy of Alan Turkus

1941

Mr. and Mrs. Chester Graham were married in Berkeley, California, on September 6, 1941.

Chester (Chet), the grandson of prominent attorney and University of California Regent Guy Chaffee Earl, was later awarded the French National Order of the Legion of Honour medal for his actions during World War II.

On the opposite page, Nancy Leland is seen with her father on her way to the wedding.

1941

The wedding of Lieutenant Frank Sherral Bissaker and Norma Sherrie Bissell in Australia

Credit: Bissaker photo from the Australian War Memorial's collection (www.awm.gov.au)

A bride poses for her wedding portrait at a Japanese internment camp during World War II in 1942 — Tule Lake War Relocation Center in Newell, California

1942

1942

War brides

Mr. & Mrs. Watson were married on June 10, 1942

Mr & Mrs Paulter were married on November 2, 1943

1947

Credit: Photo courtesy of Flickr user InAweofGod'sCreation/N Houlihan

1947

Royal Wedding

Elizabeth II and Prince Philip, Duke of Edinburgh were married on November 20, 1947 at Westminster Abbey in London. Her bridal gown, Designed by Sir Norman Hartnell, was made of ivory silk, decorated with white crystals and 10,000 seed pearls. The gown had a 15 foot star-patterned train, inspired by the famous Renaissance painting of Primavera by Botticelli (seen in inset above).

The end

Grow old with me! The best is yet to be.

– ROBERT BROWNING

Notes & thanks

Photos and illustrations have been restored as faithfully as possible, but in many cases, we relied upon high-resolution scans of the printed newspaper and magazine pages. As such, shapes and lines are occasionally incomplete, and some details have been lost due to printing processes and quality of preserved paper and negatives.

Text excerpts may have been edited for length, clarity, spelling & terminology. Text in italics denotes notes and/or historical context added by the author.

In many photographs, the subjects remain unidentified, and some dates may be estimated.

Image scans, photos and text were kindly provided by the United States Library of Congress, Google Books, Library and Archives Canada, the State Library of New South Wales (Australia), The George Eastman House, The Internet Archive, private collections and numerous other sources. Graphic design elements include those provided via Adobe, Dreamstime and Freepik.

The Robinsons and the Grahams featured inside are relatives of the author.

More vintage wedding features and much more may be found online at Click Americana (ClickAmericana.com).

ABOUT THE AUTHOR

Nancy J. Price started self-publishing music fanzines at age 14, and graduated to interviewing major-label rock bands at 16. Less than a decade later, during a three-year-stint in the music industry, she moonlighted as a freelance writer, earning bylines in *Parents* and the *San Francisco Chronicle*, among others.

Together with her best friend, Nancy co-founded Myria.com, ePregnancy.com and SheKnows.com in the late 1990s. In 2003, Nancy helped turn SheKnows.com into a top lifestyle website for women, reaching more than 30 million readers per month. Along with serving as the site's Executive Editor until 2011, Nancy helped launch three national newsstand magazines.

Though a fourth-generation San Francisco Bay Area native, Nancy now lives in Arizona. When she's not spending time with her family, reading or traveling, Nancy is perpetually creating — words, websites and various projects for print. In addition to her work on the Myria.com and ClickAmericana.com sites, she wrote a time travel novel, *Dream of Time*, created the *Vintage Women: Adult Coloring Book* series, and wrote *The All-In-One Pregnancy Calendar, Daily Countdown, Planner and Journal*.

See more at nancyjprice.com, and on Twitter (@andwhatsnext).

ABOUT THE PUBLISHER

Synchronista LLC is a boutique creative company, with a passion for website development, web design, print design and publishing, photography, writing & editing, brand creation and other media pursuits.

Published books include *The All-In-One Pregnancy Calendar, Daily Countdown, Planner and Journal*, the *Vintage Women Adult Coloring Book* series, the *Brilliant Activity Books* series, and *Dream of Time* (a novel). Current websites include ClickAmericana.com (thousands of vintage articles and images), ChoreTell.com (free printable checklists, shopping lists and chore charts), PrintColorFun.com (free printable coloring book pages) and ClickBabyNames.com. Visit Synchronista.com to find out more.